SCHOOL SHAKE-UP

HIDDEN PICTURE PUZZLES

BY
JILL KALZ

ILLUSTRATED BY
DOUGLAS HOLGATE

PICTURE WINDOW BOOKS
a capstone imprint

DESIGNER: LORI BYE
ART DIRECTOR: NATHAN GASSMAN
PRODUCTION SPECIALIST: DANIELLE CEMINSKY
THE ILLUSTRATIONS IN THIS BOOK WERE CREATED DIGITALLY.

PICTURE WINDOW BOOKS
1710 ROE CREST DRIVE
NORTH MANKATO, MN 56003
WWW.CAPSTONEPUB.COM

Library of Congress Cataloging-in-Publication Data
Kalz, Jill.
 School shake-up : hidden picture puzzles / by Jill Kalz ; illustrated
by Douglas Holgate.
    p. cm. — (Seek it out)
 Summary: "Illustrated scenes related to elementary school invite readers
to find a list of objects hidden within them"—Provided by publisher.
 ISBN 978-1-4048-7496-1 (library binding)
 ISBN 978-1-4048-7726-9 (paperback)
 ISBN 978-1-4048-7993-5 (ebook PDF)
 1. Picture puzzles—Juvenile literature. I. Holgate, Douglas, ill.
II. Title.
 GV1507.P47K35 2013
 793.73—dc23
                              2012007185

DIRECTIONS:

Look at the pictures and find the items on the lists. Not too tough, right? Not for a clever kid like you. But be warned: The first few puzzles are tricky. The next ones are even trickier. And the final puzzles are for the bravest seekers only. Good luck!

Printed in the United States of America
in Stevens Point, Wisconsin.
032012   006678WZF12

TABLE OF CONTENTS

Before the Bell

- nest
- robin
- frog
- jump rope
- trumpet
- cupcake

Ain't Band Grand?

- trophy
- paper airplane
- triangle
- button
- bow tie
- pear

6

Play Day

- coffee cup
- rattle
- thread
- hanger
- banana
- grasshopper

Soccer Surprise

- popcorn
- megaphone
- butterfly
- frog
- flower
- chipmunk

Field Trip Treasures

- headphones
- penguin
- squirrel
- fish
- binoculars
- key

Festival Fun

- bluebird
- dinosaur
- pie
- basketball
- duck
- troll

Computer Confusion

- dog
- rainbow
- violin
- fish
- star
- paper clip
- spider
- suitcase
- dragon

17

The Lunch Bunch

- orange
- calendar
- flag
- tennis ball
- grade
- spilled milk
- coyote
- balloon
- earmuffs

18

Dressed for Recess

- kickball
- polar bear
- whistle
- top hat
- earmuffs
- button
- hot chocolate
- snake
- sunglasses

21

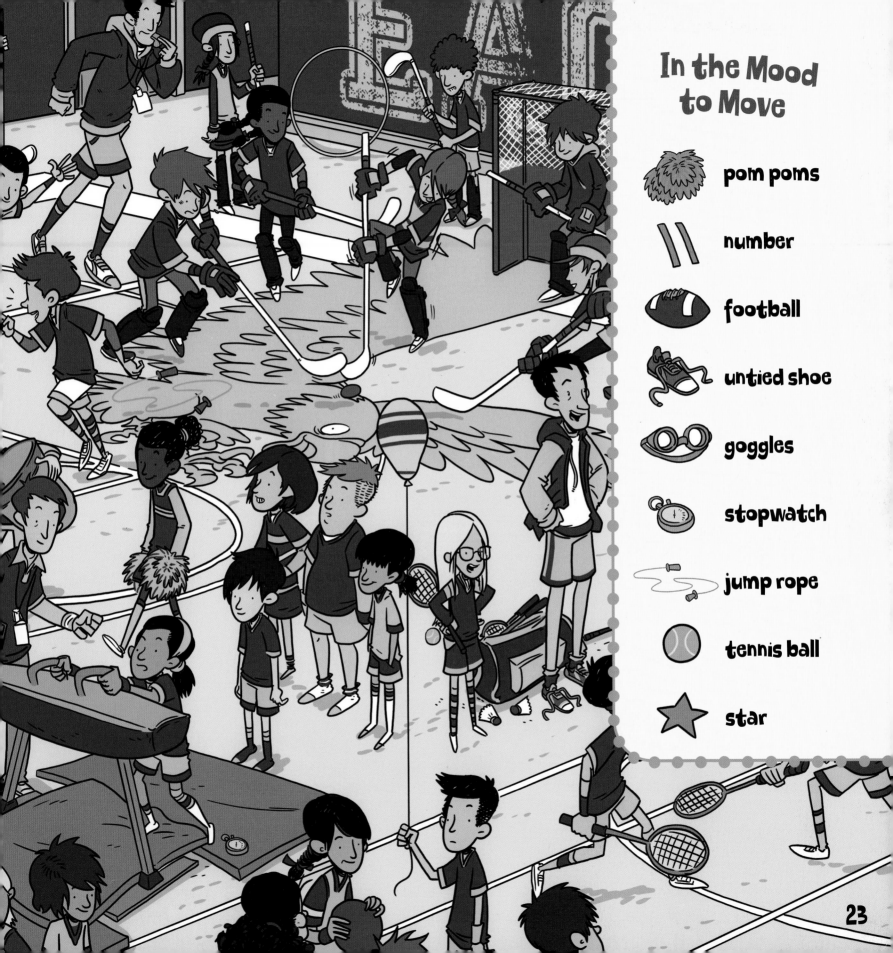

In the Mood to Move

- pom poms
- number
- football
- untied shoe
- goggles
- stopwatch
- jump rope
- tennis ball
- star

23

Pretty in Paint

- snowflake
- cookie
- ruler
- guitar
- dustpan
- flute
- parrot
- scissors
- gift

W-i-n-n-e-r!

 camera

 stopwatch

 ribbon

 flower

 popcorn

 heart

 butterfly

 star

 cap

 clover

 keys

 donut

26

Strange Science

 fish

 bat

 moth

 lightning bolt

 worm

 mouse

 cat

 broomstick

 toad

 snail

 dog bone

 thermometer

Read It!

 globe

 crocodile

 horse

 clock

 duck

 train

 cactus

 fish bowl

 umbrella

 stork

 grapes

 puppet

30

FOUND EVERYTHING?

Not quite! Flip back and see if you can find these sneaky items.

 gopher

 ice skates

 cowboy boots

 stop sign

 football helmet

toy truck

 scarecrow

 giraffe

 pencil sharpener

 thermos

Internet Sites

FactHound offers a safe, fun way to find Internet sites related to this book. All of the sites on FactHound have been researched by our staff.

Here's all you do:

Visit *www.facthound.com*

Type in this code: 9781404874961

 **Super-cool stuff!** Check out projects, games and lots more at **www.capstonekids.com**

look for all the books in the series:

CHRISTMAS CHAOS

HALLOWEEN HIDE AND SEEK

SCHOOL SHAKE-UP

ZOO HIDEOUT